Conrad K. Bu

MW01140167

THE BEST SUPERCARS
IN THE WORLD

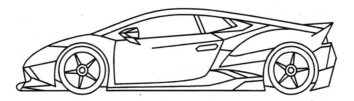

A more recent term for high-performance sportscars is "hypercar", which is sometimes used to describe the highest-performing supercars. Hypercars push the limit of their impossibility. For the absolute pinnacle of the automotive industry that exceeds the limits of the range. Everything in the hyperauts must be exaggerated and loud enough to give a signal and to the observers the impression of anxiety and excitement. Coming out of a hyperaut, you're just glad you're still alive!

Several features elevate a car to an elite level, but not all of them have to be met to be included in this group. What are these features?

Availability: As you may have guessed, a hypercar is not a vehicle that we can buy at your local dealership. Mainly because building such a hyperaut costs a lot. The most important thing is that the mass-produced car is not so unusual anymore and it does not arouse such euphoria.

Luxury: Hyperauts are created with great attention to detail, each element fits the other like Jin to Jang. They are not mass-produced by machines, but carefully and conscientiously created by people.

Performance: The most important of these three characteristics. Each supercar has an amazing performance. And they decide that this vehicle can be called that. Top speed, high torque, acceleration, precise handling.

So what exactly are hypercars, the best of the best supercars? The first undisputed hyperauto was the 2005 Bugatti Veyron.

Of course, there are voices that the first such car - and in a way rightly - was, for example, the Ferrari F40, but what Bugatti offered exceeded all expectations.

From the outside, the Veyron cannot be mistaken for another car: Huge air intakes protruding above the roof, A silhouette with a round and muscular shape - these are the distinguishing features of this model.

The interior of the Veyron is full of luxury. A wide range of color configurations was available. All elements are trimmed with leather, and the finishing touches are made with great care.

The 16-cylinder W-shape engine with quadruple-turbo charging and a displacement of 8 liters develops 1001 hp and 1250 Nm of torque. The Veyron became the first series-produced car to exceed 400 kmh (258 mph). Bugatti has also set an acceleration record of 0 to 100 kmh (60 mph): Veyron 16.4 needs only 2.5 seconds for this.

Lamborghini Centenario

770 horsepower monster!

In March 2016, during the Geneva Motor Show, Lamborghini presented another model from a series of limited, low-series models.
The Centenario was created as a special structure to celebrate the 100th anniversary of the birth of the founder of the Italian company, Ferruccio Lamborghini.

The Lamborghini Centenario is an uncompromising machine. The body made entirely of carbon fiber, of course, is reminiscent of the Aventador. Smooth and aggressive lines have been swept from the surface of the bodywork and replaced with extremely aggressive cuts and air intakes.

The interior is typical of a Lamborghini –
it looks out of this planet!

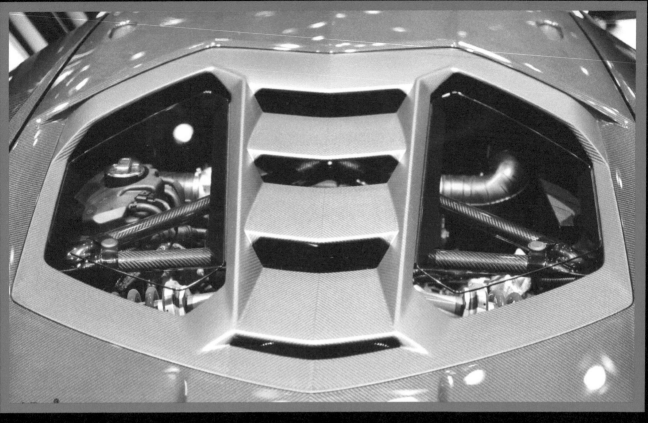

The V12 engine has a capacity of 6.5 liters and a power of 770 HP. The unit accelerates to 100 kmh (60 mph) in 2.8 seconds, developing a top speed of 350 kmh (217 mph)!

Pagani Huayra

the dream car of automotive enthusiasts

Huayra is the second sports car of the Italian manufacturer Pagani. The first copies of this car left a small manufacture located in Modena in 2011. The name comes from the South American God of wind - Huayra-tata,

At the front, double round lights are mounted in elliptical carbon fiber inserts. A sharp, triangular nose cuts the huge maw on the front strip. At the rear, you can admire the four exhaust tips placed in a circular opening.

The entire interior has a classic, elegant style, but thanks to the colorful, touchscreen display and the ubiquitous carbon fiber, it is phenomenal. The seats and parts of the dashboard and side panels are made of high-quality genuine leather.

It is powered by a centrally located V12 6.0-liter Twin-Turbo V12 unit from Mercedes-AMG, generating a maximum power of 730 hp. Top speed is 378 kmh (235 mph) and acceleration is 0-100 kmh (60 mph) in 3.3 seconds.

Koenigsegg One:1

The car was built to break the record for the maximum speed of a mass-produced car

The name of this amazing model comes from two technical parameters: the power-to-weight ratio, which is exactly 1: 1 (1 horsepower of power corres ponds to 1 kilogram of vehicle weight) and the engine power of 1 megawatt (the manufacturer describes One: 1 as "the world's first" Megacar ").

Koenigsegg One: 1 is equipped with very advanced aerodynamics. It makes the car not only the king of straight lines, but also a precise machine for cornering. The side overloads achieved by One: 1 are even 2G, which is a result more known from airplanes than from cars traveling on public roads. To achieve this result, the car was equipped with a large front splitter and a movable two-piece wing at the rear.

Koenigsegg One: 1 was made of the best materials. Inside, we have a symmetrical, minimalist aesthetic and an ocean of carbon. The center console looks like it comes from a spaceship...

The car's parameters are amazing. The proprietary 5-liter
V8 engine develops 1360 hp and generates a torque of 1371 Nm.
The performance of this megascar beats everything you have seen so
far. The car accelerates to 400 kmh (248 mph) in just 20 seconds!

Porsche 918 Spyder

successor to the legendary Carrera GT

The Porsche 918 Spyder is a production version of the car that was first presented as a concept in 2010. The enthusiastic reception of the visitors to the Geneva motor show made Porsche decided to prepare the serial production of this car.

The body of the 918 Spyder consists of panels made of plastics and reinforced composite fibers. They combine lightness with relatively high durability. Interesting idea is the two exhaust pipes led out above the engine. This is the only solution of this type in the automotive industry.

The interior of the Porsche is quite ascetic and is dominated by a rather small steering wheel and a central panel with a large touchscreen. There are two knobs below. The steering wheel is equipped with gearshift paddles and buttons for controlling the car's operating modes. The dashboard itself is dominated by a tachometer.

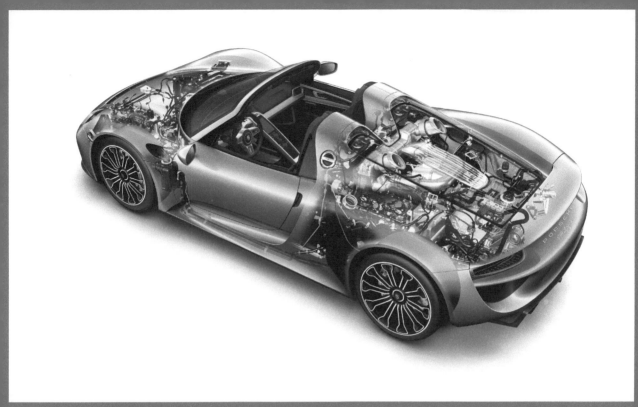

The total power of the system consisting of the electric / combustion kit is 887 hp at 8,500 rpm, and the maximum torque ranges from 917 Nm to 1,280 Nm. The super hybrid from 0 to 100 kmh (60 mph) accelerates in 2.6 seconds. Top speed is 345 kmh (214 mph).

McLaren Senna

presented at the end of 2017 is a car which the manufacturer himself describes as extreme

The Senna is a high-performance supercar built as an alternative to the smaller 570S and 720S models with a more road character. The name of the racing model is a McLaren tribute to the titled Brazilian racing driver Ayrton Senna, who died tragically during a race at Imola in 1994.

The engineers spent two years working on the carbon fiber body itself, which resulted in the creation of the most durable monokock in the history of the British brand. The car weighs only 1198 kg. You won't find too many unnecessary elements here. Even the brake discs are surprisingly light - they

The interior is raw and minimalistic. The constructors boast that the entire equipment (interior) weighs only 60 kilograms (132 ibs). Special bucket seats will take you into the world like from F1 bolid.

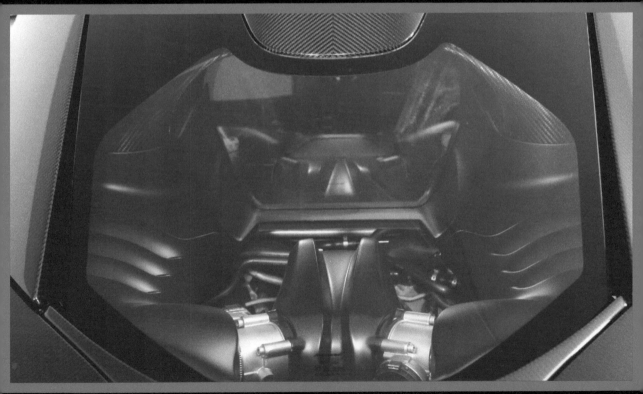

The four-liter, double-supercharged V8 engine produces 800 horsepower and produces 800 Newton meters of torque. The car weighs only 1,198 kg (2 641 ibs), so it accelerates to 100 kmh (60 mph) in just 2.8 seconds. Top speed is 340 kmh (211 mph).

Ferrari LaFerrari

spiritual successor to the F40, F50 and Enzo

Unveiled at the Geneva Motor Show in spring 2013, the LaFerrari was the fastest Ferrari road model ever. It is the first supercar of the Italian brand to be equipped with a hybrid drive.

As befits a top Ferrari model, LaFerrari has a silhouette that stands out even from Ferrari. The car has a fairly long front overhang and an extremely short rear overhang. The passenger compartment is heavily forward, which is why the engine is centrally located. The LaFerrari chassis is a composite monocoque with a carbon fiber body attached to it.

Fernando ALONSO

The passenger compartment is typical of a Ferrari - there is nothing in it that is not needed by the driver or passenger while traveling. The bucket seats are covered with leather, and the steering wheel - typically in Ferrari - is "crushed" at the top and bottom. The gears are shifted using paddles on the steering wheel.

The car was equipped with a 6.3-liter V12 engine with 800 hp and a 163 hp electric motor. The total power of the vehicle is 963 KM. This absolutely amazing car takes 2.4 seconds to accelerate to 100 kmh (60 mph). The top speed of the Italian car is approximately 350 km / h (217 mph).

Check also:

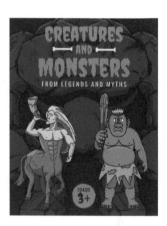

and much more!

Printed in the USA
CPSIA information can be obtained
at www.ICGtesting.com
LVHW062341171223
766737LV00003B/93